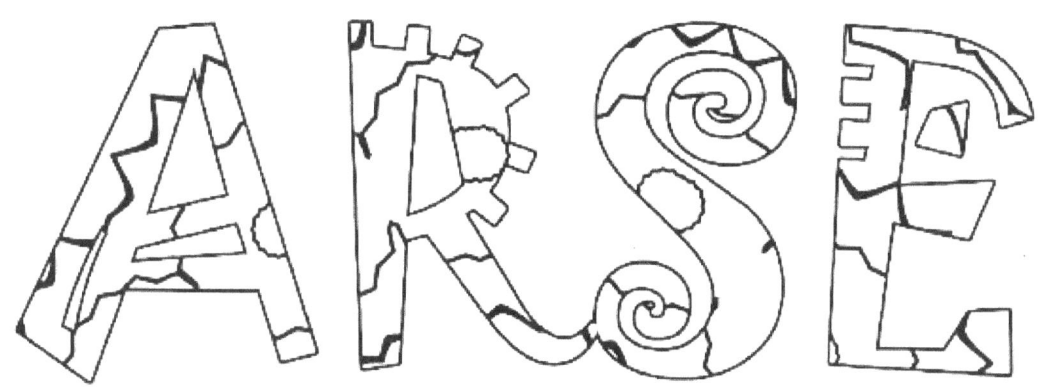

ARSE

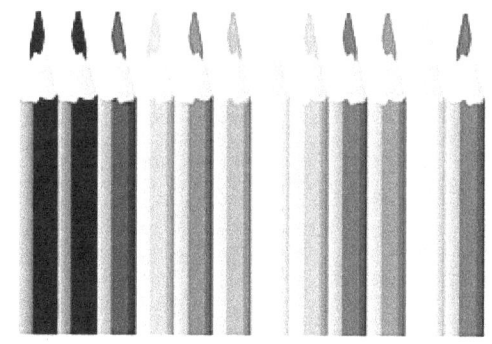

SWEAR WORD
ADULT COLORING

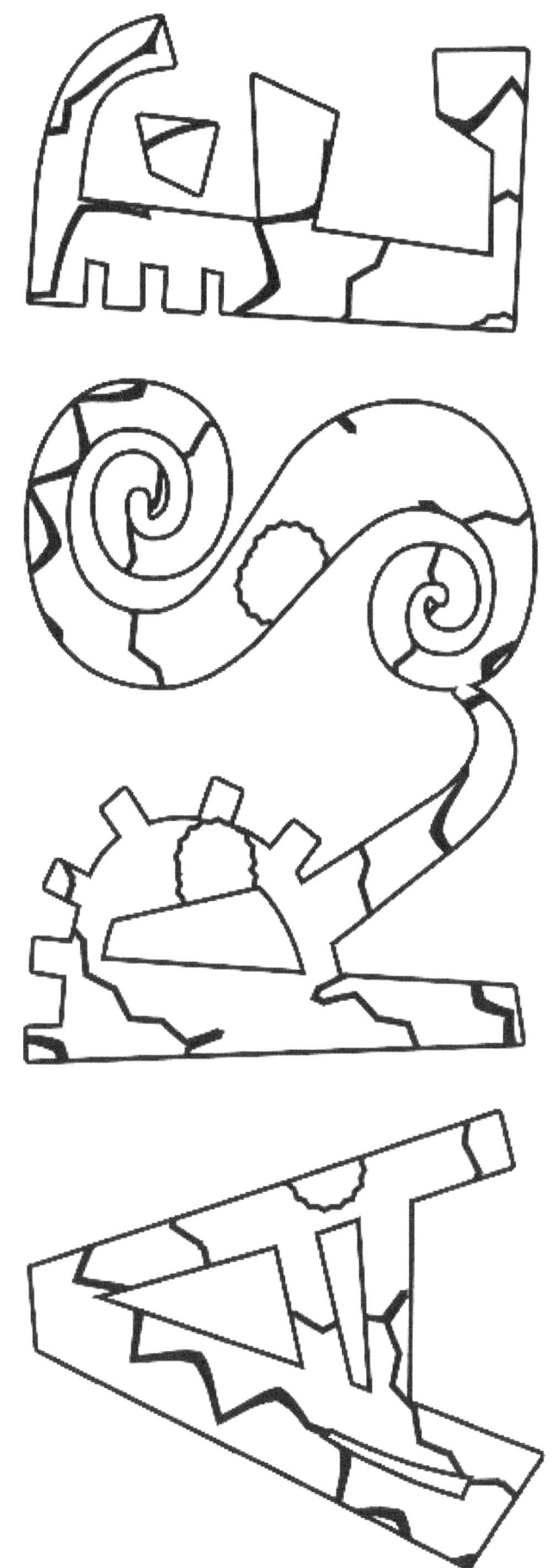

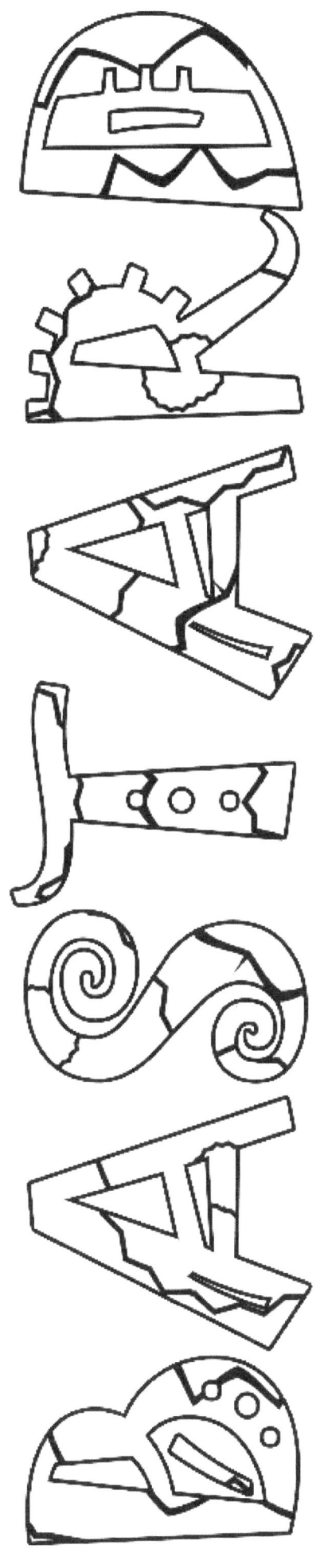

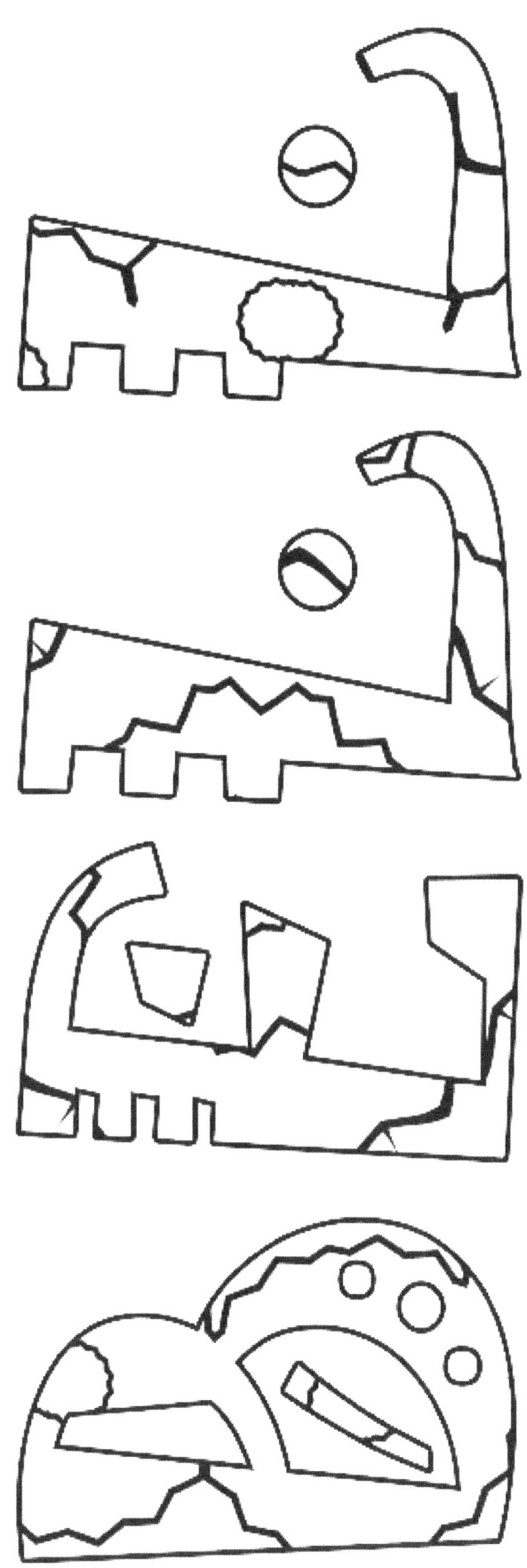

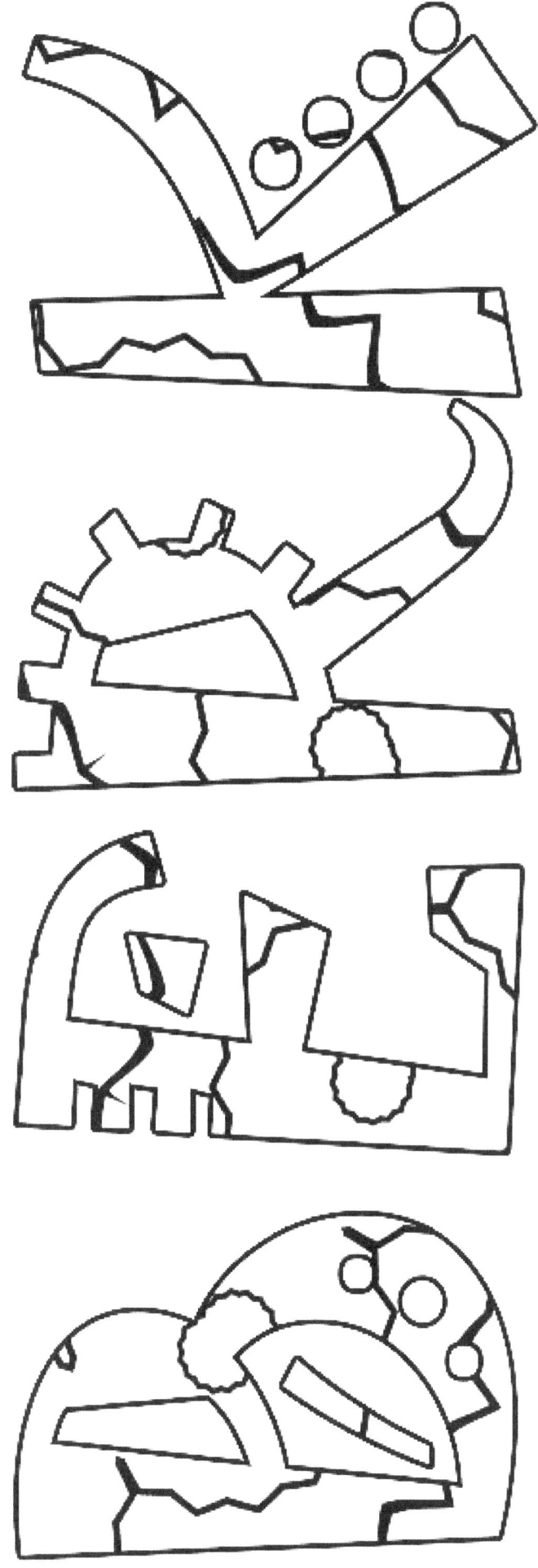

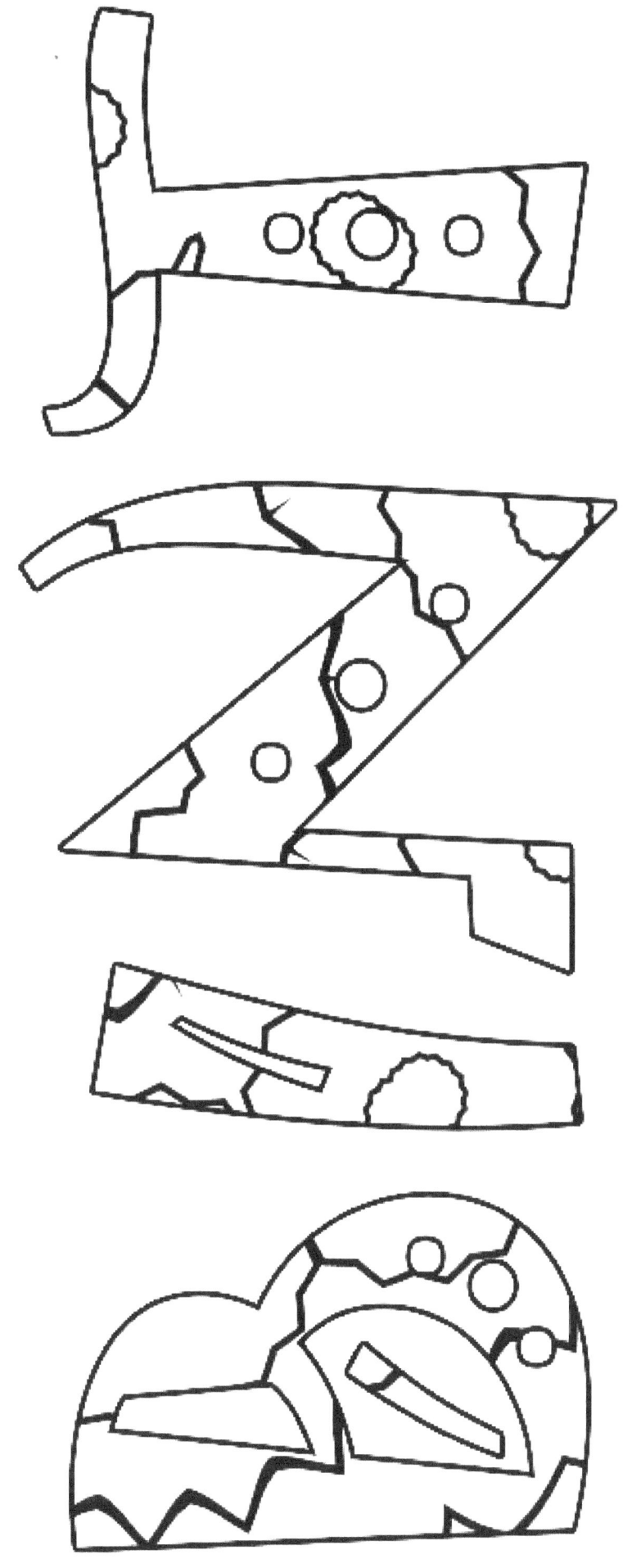

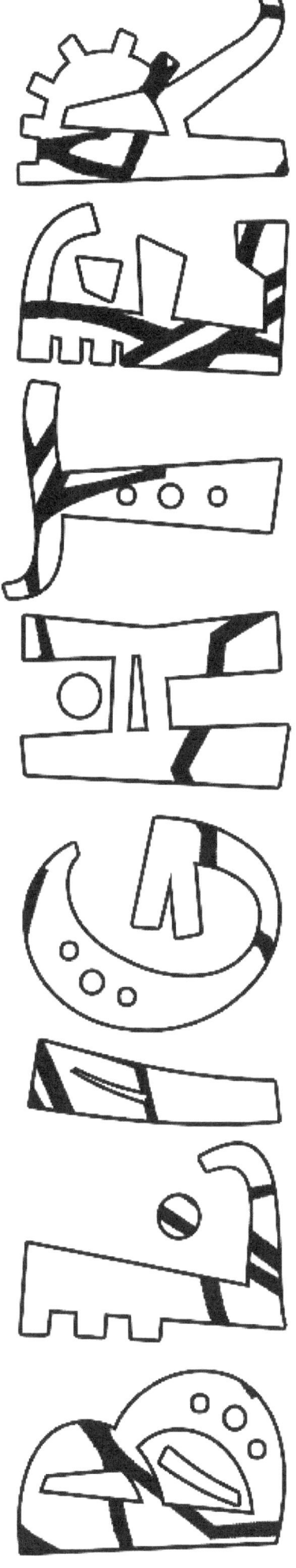

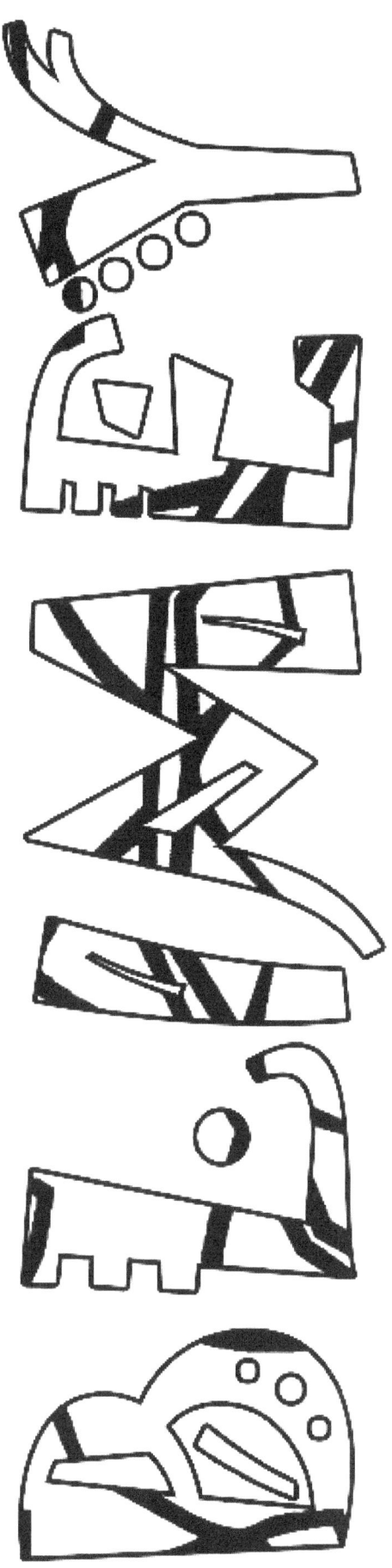

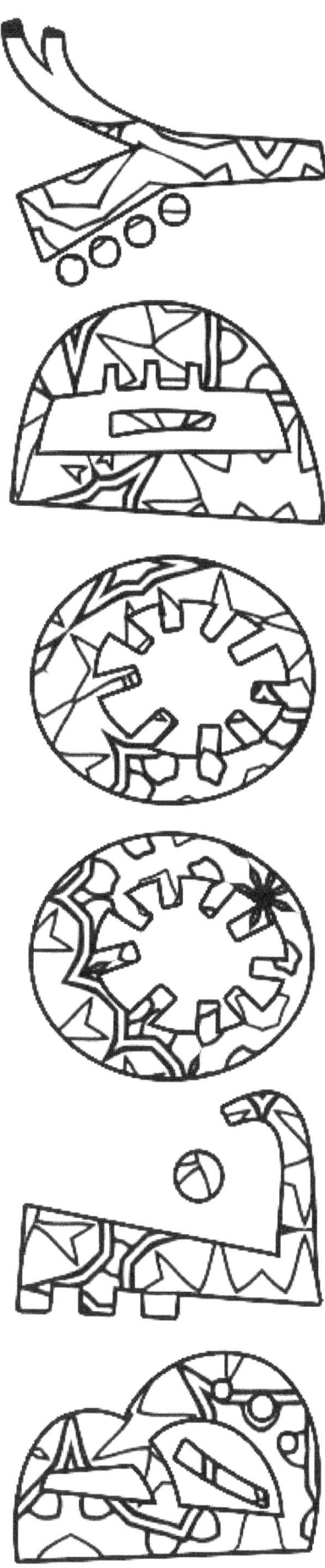

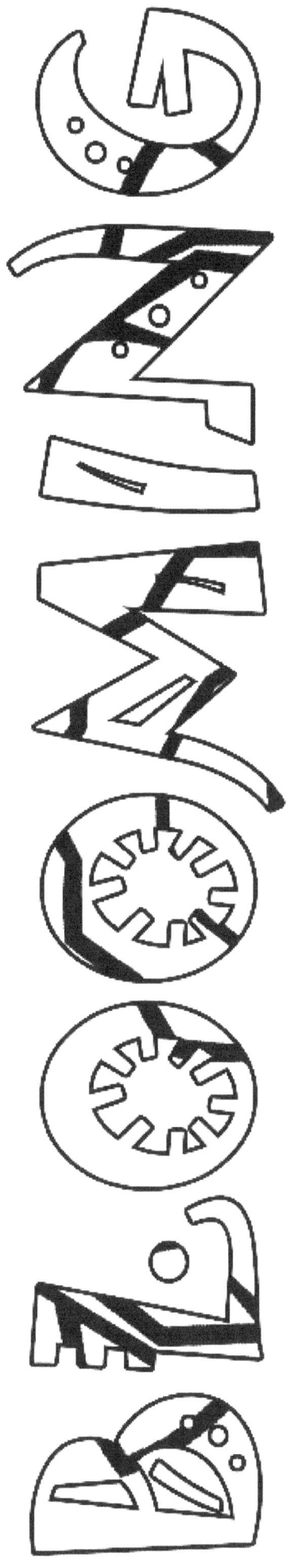

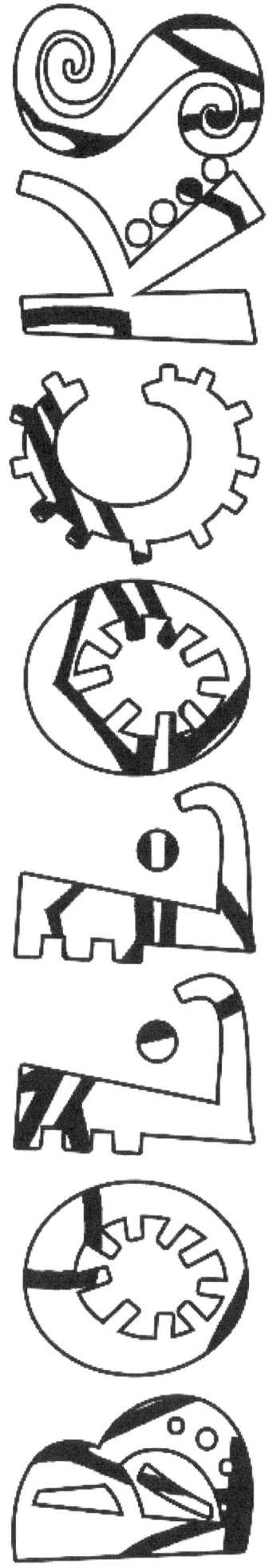

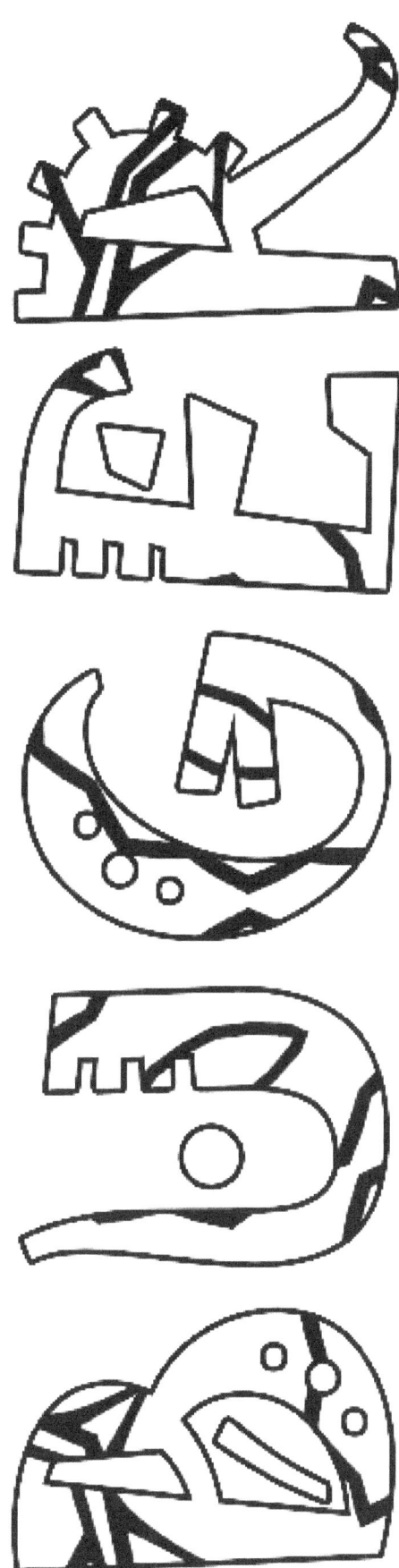

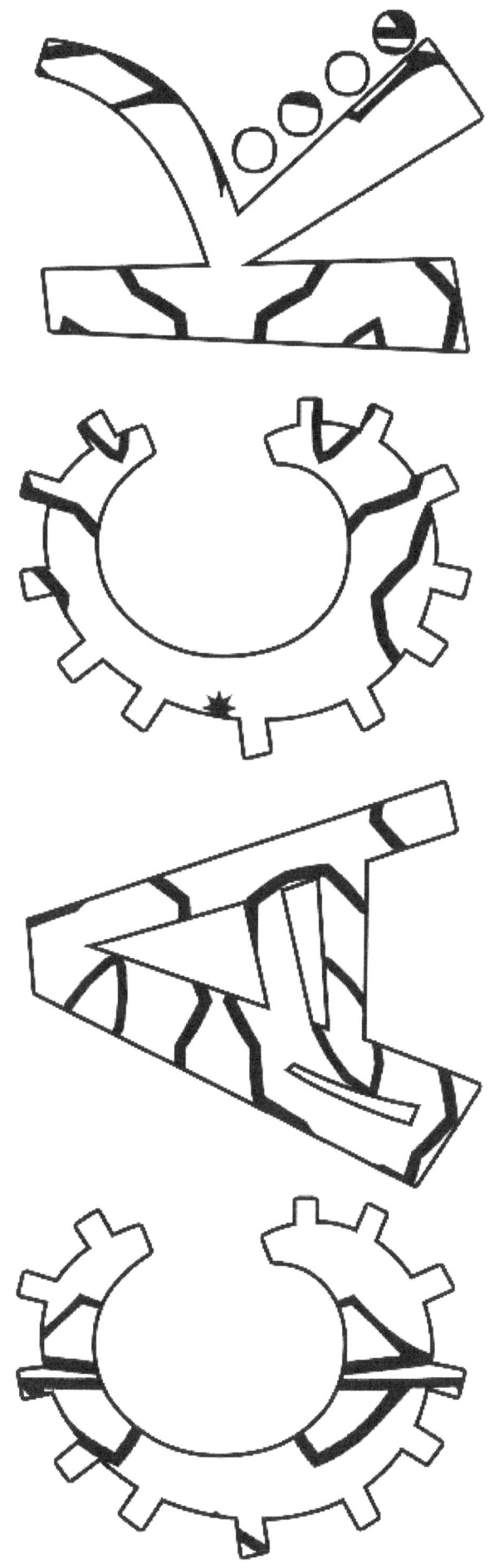

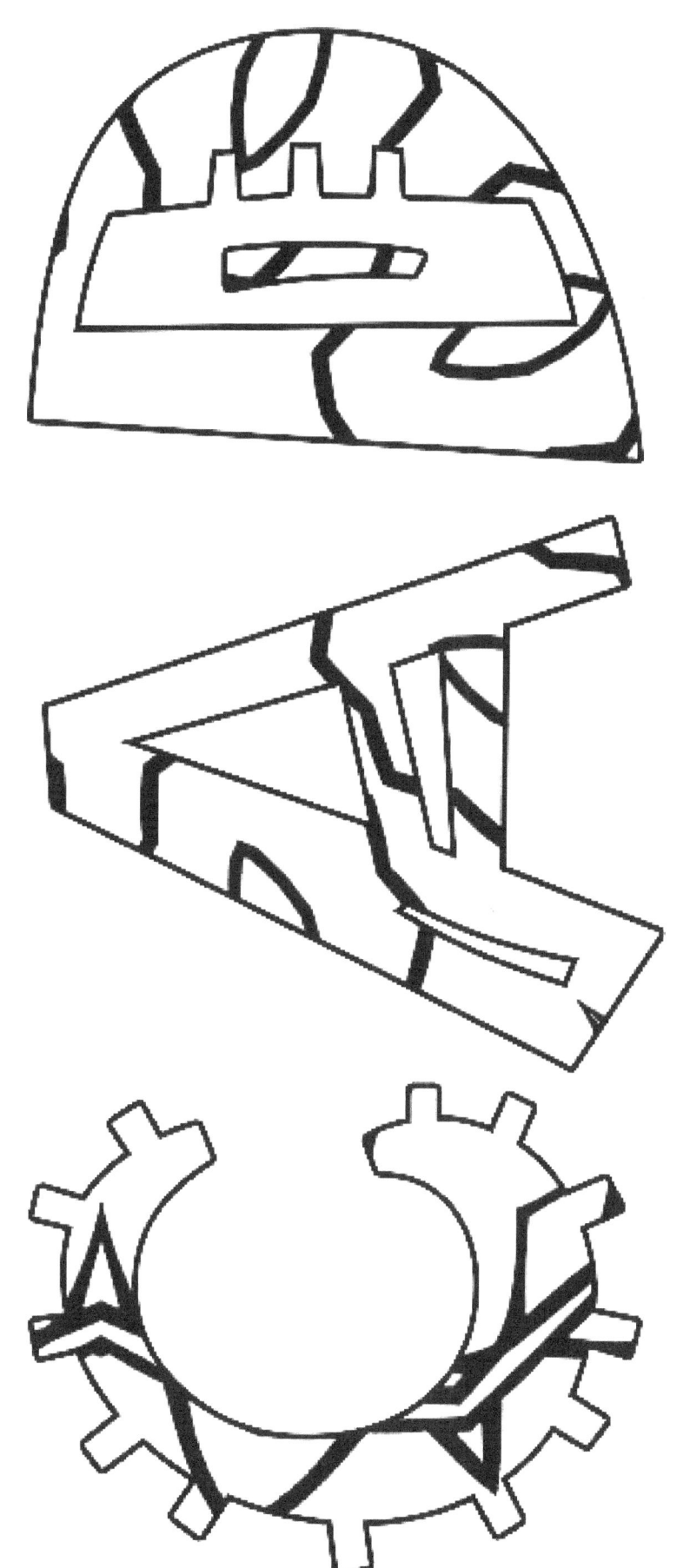

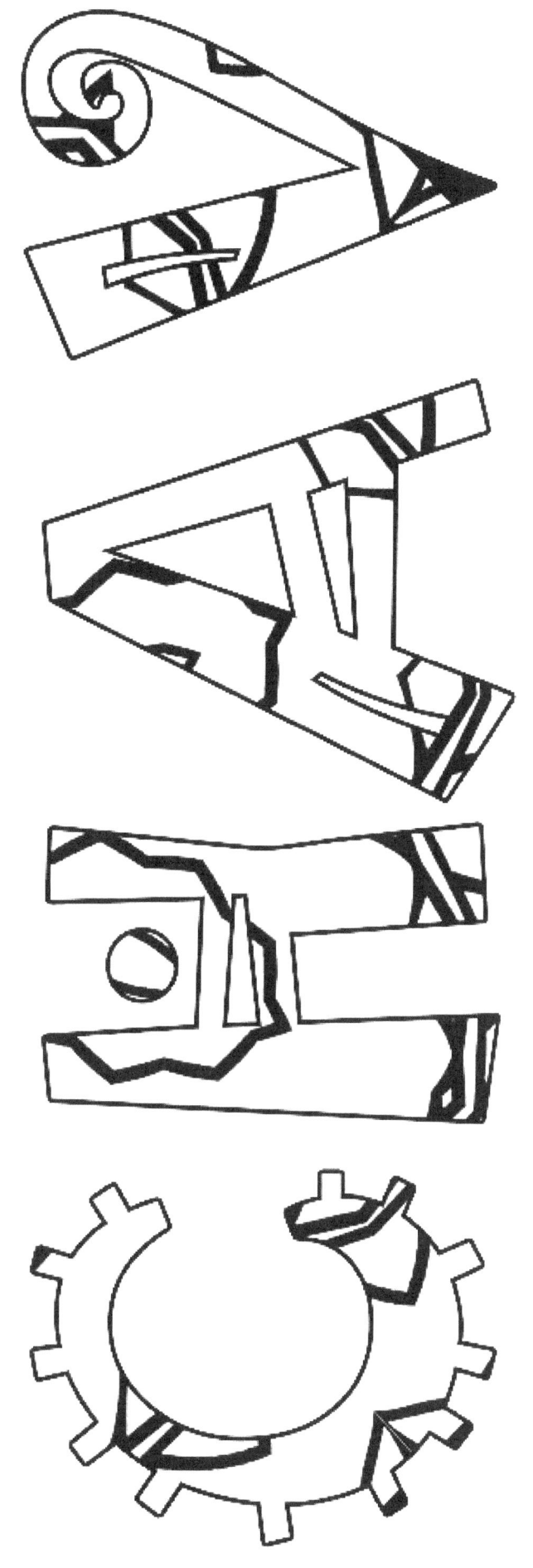

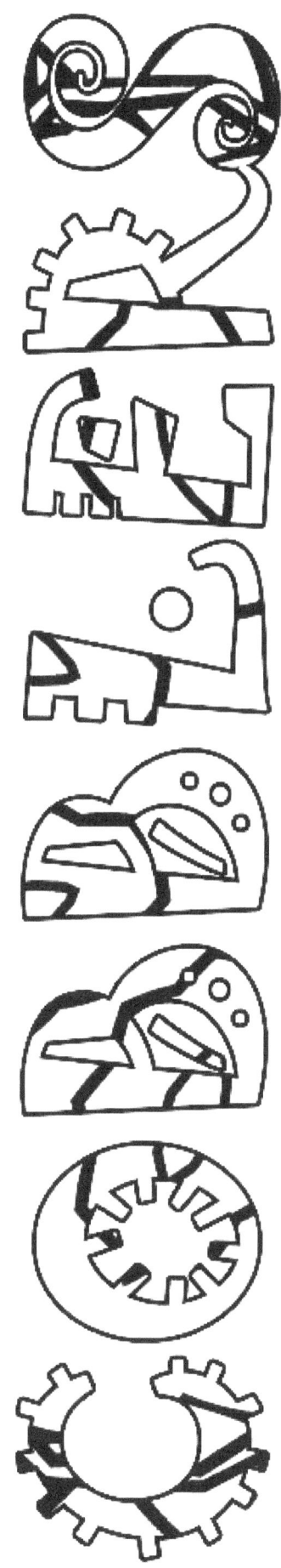

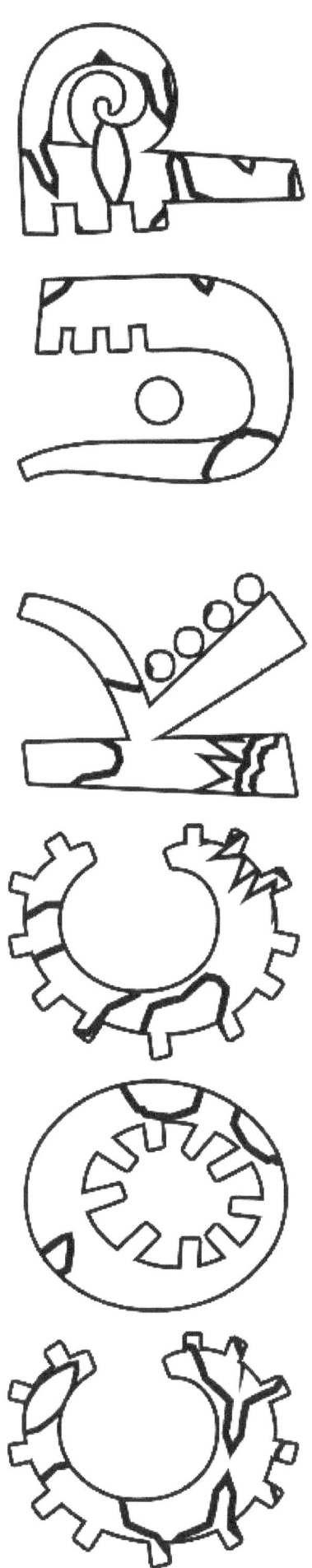

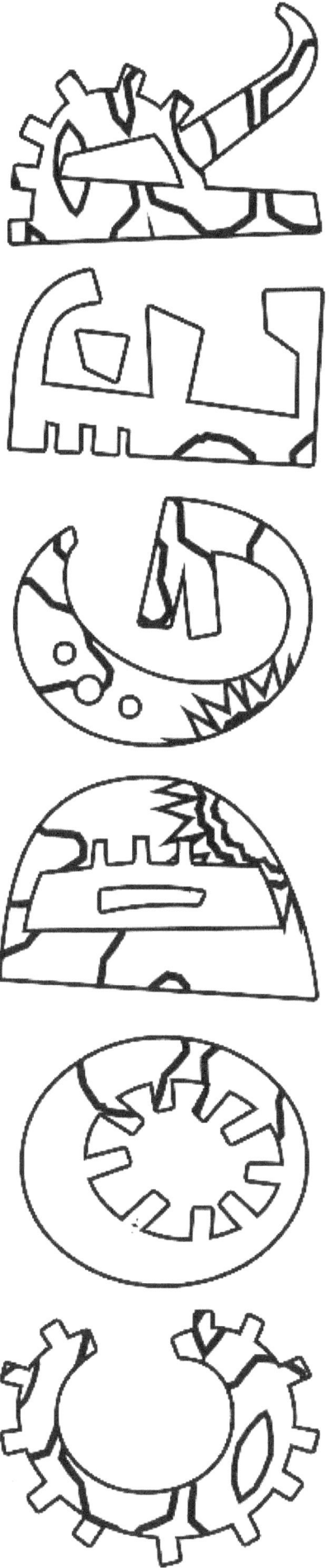

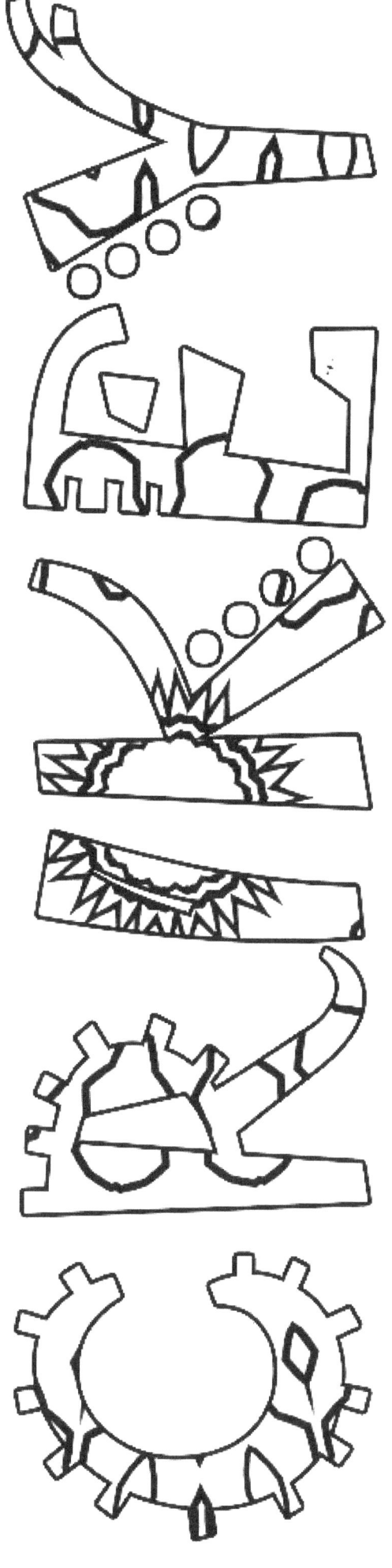

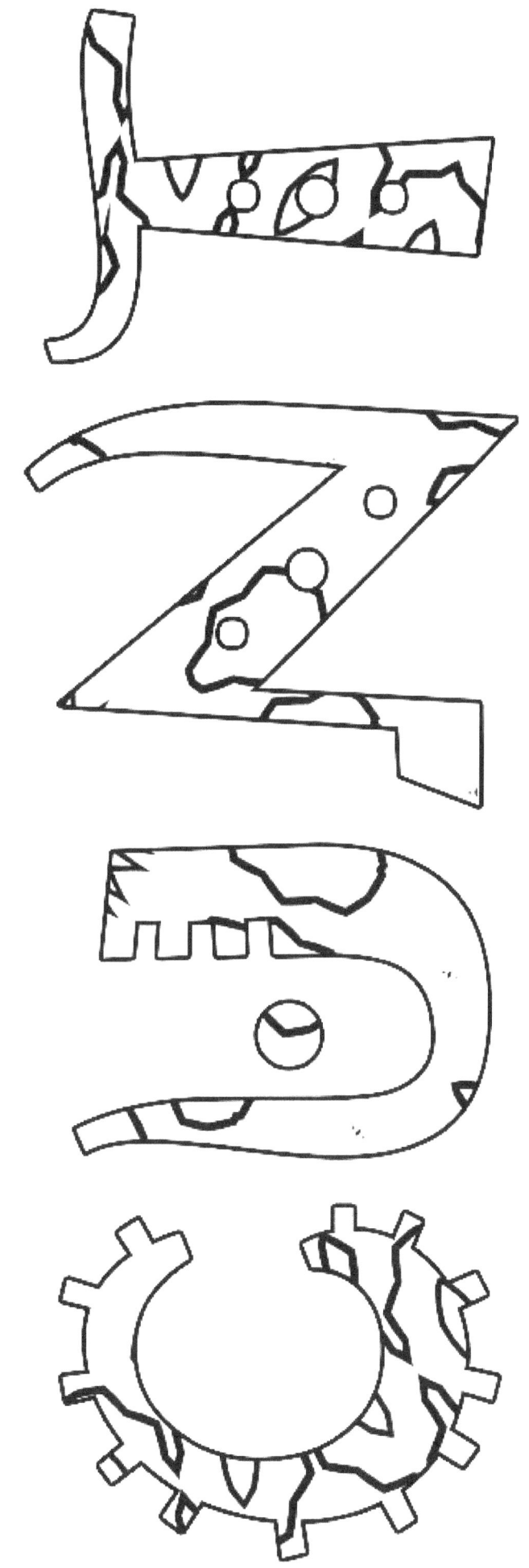

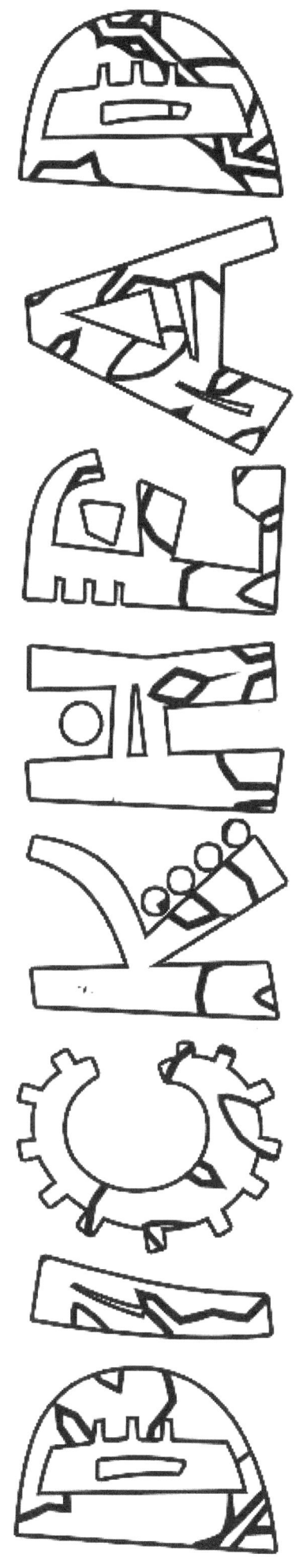

DID YOU KNOW?

* Authors are not rich. In fact, most make less than $10, 000 a year. Being an author is a SMALL BUSINESS

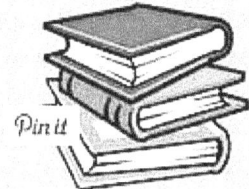

* If there are 50 reviews, Amazon lists a book in its newsletters and other promotions (Also Boughts)

* REVIEWS are the easiest way to say THANK YOU to an author and tell their publisher to produce more books.

* Reviews can be short: "I LIKED IT". It's the number of reviews that matters the most.

SUPPORT AUTHORS
SUPPORT SMALL
BUSINESS

www.tallpoppies.org

www.ingramcontent.com/pod-product-compliance
Lightning Source LLC
Chambersburg PA
CBHW080643190526
45169CB00009B/3481